ST. MARY'S C
ST. MARY'S C

W9-BQM-146

REFLECTIONS of a PALESTINIAN

Mohammad Tarbush

THIS BOOK WAS DONATED BY
THE AMERICAN EDUCATIONAL TRUST
PUBLISHER OF THE WASHINGTON
REPORT ON MIDDLE EAST AFFAIRS
BOX 53062 WASHINGTON DC 20009

American-Arab Affairs Council
Washington, DC

First published in 1986

American-Arab Affairs Council
1730 M Street, NW, Suite 512
Washington, DC 20036
Telephone, (202) 296-6767
Telex, 440506 AMARA UI

© American-Arab Affairs Council, 1986

Library of Congress Catalog Card
Number 85-73827

ISBN 0-943182-04-2

For five outstanding Arab philanthropists:

Hamad Ben Abdul-Rahman al-Hinti
Zain Mayasi
Walid Kattan
Omar Aggad
Mohammad Imran Bamieh

CONTENTS

INTRODUCTION

The personal and national horrors inflicted in four bloody decades of the Arab-Israeli conflict have masked the basic humanity of both parties. As Palestinians and Israelis have pressed their conflicting claims to the same land, American onlookers have by and large reserved their identification of underlying humanness to one side of the issue. It has therefore become difficult for them to recognize or accept the root causes of the conflict and the need to address them.

The American public urgently needs to be inculcated with a sense of the human perspective underpinning the Palestinians' will to survive as a national entity, uniquely comparable to that of the Jews. This task is difficult, in part due to the American media, which, preoccupied with the tactics of warfare and its strategic implications, for the most part lag far behind the Europeans in their approach to the unresolved status of the Palestinians. That some of the most prestigious newspapers in the West—*The Times* of London, *Le Monde, The Guardian, The International Herald Tribune, The Observer*—have published the writings of Mohammad Tarbush over the last fourteen years is evidence of their effort to promote open discussion of the issue at the heart of Arab-Israeli conflict. Successive Israeli governments have tried to show that this disparity in American and European attitudes about the Middle East stems from Europe's being held "hostage" to Arab oil, a facile explanation which unfortunately has proven readily adaptable to journalistic reductionism in this country. Well before OPEC took effective control of the international oil market, the Europeans and their media seemed responsive to something that is still under-appreciated here: namely, that the unresolved status of the Palestinians is at the bottom of Arab-Israeli hostility and suspicion.

The selected letters and articles which follow, notwithstanding their obvious political content, are basically an expression of personal anguish which arises from a stark realization: Palestinian nationalism is poised to fall through the cracks in a world system that is apparently eager to hasten its disappearance. It would be more convenient for the rest of the world if the Palestinians simply accepted the status quo. Although the author does not spare the Arab world, where some of what he sees undermines human progress and values, he views the primary challenge to Palestinian identity to be Israel and Zionism.

For many years the author's thesis has been that while Zionism as a political philosophy may have been effective in attracting Jewish immigrants to Palestine and Israel, it is a "dead end" as a humane or practical guide to governing a heterogeneous society. It should be noted that many Israelis have themselves for some time been conceding the point Mr. Tarbush has sought to make. In an essay on the effect of Israel's occupation of Arab territories since 1967, *Washington Post* correspondent William Claiborne reported that Israelis were openly questioning "whether ruling the lives of 1.4 million occupied Arabs has not, in a way, poisoned the soul and psyche of Israeli society and desensitized a people whose religion, after all, is based on humanism. . . .The nation seems at odds with itself and its values, and the Zionist vision appears somehow to have gone out of focus with a corrosive blend of cynicism and despair that penetrates every level of society." It is a bitterly poignant irony that this assessment was published on June 6, 1982, literally on the eve of Israel's invasion of Lebanon, an event which clearly has exacerbated the crisis of Zionism in Israel.

Mr. Tarbush's writing reveals his personal odyssey from one country to another, through the experiences of university life in London and Oxford, and on to a professional career based in Paris. Each change in domicile noted in the following selection of articles and letters represents a milestone in his own history and conveys much about the times in which we live. The beginnings of this odyssey are laid out in the essay "Home Thoughts from Abroad," in which the author describes life as it used to be in the Palestinian village of Beit Natif. Because it so clearly draws the frame in which Mr. Tarbush's reflections as a Palestinian are permanently couched, this article (dated July 1976) was selected to begin the collection.

Anger and despair are most vividly expressed in the pieces written shortly after the Israeli invasion of Lebanon, particularly after the massacre of hundreds of Palestinians, including scores of women and children, at the refugee camps of Sabra and Chatila. This was the nadir of modern Palestinian experience, hardening the psychological barrier which must be overcome if peace is ever to be realized.

The reflections contained in this volume are an effort by a humane conscience to reach beyond this barrier. It is to be hoped that Americans, who in recent years have experienced humiliations of their own in the Middle East, will reach out from behind their barrier and identify a kindred spirit in Mohammad Tarbush.

Frederick W. Axelgard
Fellow in Middle East Studies
Center for Strategic and International Studies
Georgetown University
Washington, D.C.
May 1986

PREFACE

As a Palestinian who has been living in Europe for the last twenty years, I can discern a striking similarity between the handling by the American media of the Palestinian problem and the way it used to be handled by the European media in the late 1960s. At that time, there was rarely a reference to the fact that Israel was built on the systematic and premeditated destruction of Palestinian homes and farms, that room was made for the incoming Jewish immigrants by chasing hundreds of thousands of Palestinians out of their land, that terrorism developed as a peculiarly Zionist speciality—in short, that Israel came into existence by the negation of the Palestinians and their right to nationhood.

Israel was commonly perceived as a modern state struggling for its own security. Its oppressive practices against those Palestinians who managed to stay on after the creation of the state in 1948, and Israel's aggression against its Arab neighbors were invariably ignored or excused. Its refusal to allow the Palestinian refugees to return to their homes was also accepted, or at best left unchallenged.

Happily, where Europe is concerned there is now a general recognition of the injustices committed against the Palestinians, and with time I am sure that there will be growing voices calling for the redemption of these injustices. The European media, particularly the press, no longer shy away from giving comprehensive coverage to Israeli violations of human rights, particularly to cases of torture of Palestinian prisoners and unlawful confiscation of land and property.

Such treatment of the Palestinian problem by the American media is still rare and from my observations appears to be confined to a handful of newspaper, radio and television reporters. Israel's use of American-made and supplied cluster bombs and other prohibitive and prohibited weapons against neighboring civilians has never become a public issue in the United States. Pictures of maimed Palestinian mothers and children do not haunt the average American. Rather, in the United States, it is common for a discussion of the Palestinian problem, to casually drift into a presentation of stereotyped images of the Arabs and a pathetically superficial understanding of their society and culture.

The Arabs, like other people, do not live in a perfect world. As is mentioned in one of the following articles, the Arabs have their fair share of regimes lacking in legitimacy. Suppression of basic freedoms is still widely practiced in some parts of the heterogeneous Arab world. All of this however does not justify confusing the people with their un-elected regimes, and nothing could ever excuse committing a flagrant injustice against a people on the pretext that they do not have a democratically elected government. The average Arab is more unhappy about the absence of true democracy in some parts of the Arab world than any outsider can ever be, and many have risked their freedoms, sometimes their lives, in order to make their disagreements known. It is as wrong to victimize Palestinian Arabs because some Arab countries have autarchic regimes as it would be to react to Israel's oppression of the Palestinians by persecuting Jews in other parts of the world. And then, in the haze of prejudices and counter-prejudices, let it not be missed that, like others, the Palestinians are made of flesh and blood, their children feel the agony of pain as intensely as they enjoy the glow of happiness.

It is tragic that so many well-meaning Americans seem to have fallen victim to Israel's dehumanising campaigns against the Palestinians. I hope that the following articles will be viewed as genuine reactions of an ordinary Palestinian to the dramatic events which have befallen his people. They are not meant to promote any particular party or ideology; rather they are the words of a human being at times talking to none other than his own conscience.

M.T.

3

"Home Thoughts from Abroad," *Middle East International*, London (July 1976).

OXFORD—I was born in the village of Beit-Natif before it was occupied by the Zionists in 1948. I suppose that childhood impressions leave a strong imprint and I certainly remember the village vividly. Certain sounds or aromas, seemingly minor details, will suddenly bring it all back, that time of mystery and excitement. I suppose we are privileged that Beit Natif was at least large enough to appear on maps of Palestine. I wonder what it is like for those Palestinians from villages so small they do not even have the comfort of being able to look at the map and say to themselves "There it is, *my* village," who must start to doubt its exact position and might even think it was all a dream.

Our village lay in the heart of Palestine exactly halfway between the coast of the Mediterranean and the Dead Sea, just where the Judean hills start to trail off into the rich plains that stretch to the Mediterranean. From Bethlehem, you took a narrow road that twisted through the quiet cone-shaped hills encircled with terraces of white stone, where the vine clawed up through the dark rust-red earth. Gradually the road started to descend to a wide valley filled with lush greenness where much of the land belonging to the village lay. To get to the village itself you would have continued up a twisting path, until you came to the hilltop. And in a house on the outskirts of the village, near a great mulberry tree, we lived with my grandparents. Grandfather had built the house in the early years of the century and it looked onto the farmyard where the chickens strutted and pecked ceaselessly and around which were the stables for the sheep and goats. The neighboring houses were occupied by other members of the family, and I was surrounded by affection and spoilt by my many aunts.

The houses were simple in design, based on a cubic shape with shallowly domed roofs and arched doors and windows. They were ideally suited to the extremes of weather, and to enter our house in summer was like plunging into a well, so cool was the interior. Yet these houses were sturdy enough to withstand the worst batterings of winter, when raw winds often blew for days at a time, fighting ceaselessly with the trees. Winter was the time of storms, when the sky would suddenly darken and the animals became uneasy before a savage onslaught that might last for hours, thunder crashing through the hills and rattling the doors like chattering teeth, while the whole sky lit up in spasms of naked pink. After rain we would emerge to a gentle sky and a land that looked as if it had been freshly painted, everything glowing and a lovely aroma rising from the steaming earth.

Snow always came in the winter, and it was not uncommon for us to be confined to the house for days on end. But we welcomed the winter, for the rains and melting snow filled the wells with fresh supplies of water, and we kept warm enough in our snug house with olive branches crackling in the hearth, filling the house with a seeping warmth and spicy odour. Taking me on his knee, grandfather would make out scenes with me in the flames and glowing logs. We would roast nuts and I would eat them still hot, singeing my impatient fingers.

From the windows of the room I shared with my brother we looked down into the courtyard with its whitewashed walls and tiled floor. In one corner was the gate into the street, in the other was a specially built small shed where my own goat was kept. This goat had been given to me by a friend of my father's when she was very tiny, and at first I carried her everywhere. But evenutally her little hooves grew too sharp, and she repaid my affections with kicks and butts. Thus, reluctantly, I allowed her to graduate to the slaughterhouse. I used to go out early in the morning, the air still damp with night, to rummage in the straw for eggs. The chickens would squawk as my little hands interrupted their dignified squatting, and I would carefully place the warm heavy eggs in a basket, feathers and straw still sticking to them, then run back to the house.

We would wake to the call of the imam, very early in the morning. His sound often swam into my dreams becoming confused with them, until I awakened to mother shaking me. I would stumble out of bed while the adults of the family were already at prayer, each individually kneeling and performing the ritual movements on the prayer mats. After prayers came milking, at which I usually helped, lifting the latch and running over the farmyard to the stables, the air still damp with night making me shiver. Only when the animals had been cleaned out, the milking done and the eggs gathered in did we sit down to breakfast. Our diet was simple, all our food being home-produced; there was yoghurt and soft cheese, plump olives and various kinds of vegetables and fruit. Anything that needed baking was cooked in the *taboun,* a small outhouse into whose floor a circular cover was set concealing a pebble-lined chamber where the flattened dough or earthenware pots of food were laid. When the cover had been replaced a fire would be lit over it. Bread from the *taboun* was always dimpled from lying on pebbles, and had a specially delicious taste and texture. I remember how mother and grandmother used to gossip away happily as they baked the bread, shooing me and my brother out of the way as we tried to snatch pieces off those crisp loaves as they emerged, hot and golden. The floor of the *taboun* became covered with powdery white ash and had to be swept out frequently—I still remember the acrid smell of those ashes.

By the time breakfast was over, the village would be coming to life, and a bustle of people's feet and voices would start to echo in the streets.

Foreword to *Palestine or Israel* [a pictorial booklet published in May 1971].

DURHAM — Most people outside the Middle East cannot understand why the struggle between the Arabs and the Israelis has gone on for so long. Why, they ask, cannot the Arabs recognise that Israel is here to stay and get down to solving their urgent social and economic problems? Why is so much material wealth and capital wasted on bitter and apparently hopeless fighting? What is so easily overlooked by those outside the struggle is that Israel came into existence as a state by the displacement of a whole people — the Palestinian Arabs. How did this come about?

This pictorial statement tells a story which goes back to 1917, when the British Foreign Secretary, Lord Balfour, promised support for the creation of a Jewish National Home in Palestine. Palestine was then part of the Ottoman Empire. Encouraged by Britain, Jews from all over the world flooded into Palestine. Zionism appeared as a new nationalist movement and was supported by wealthy Jews in the major Western countries. The Fascist persecution of the European Jews evoked sympathy from Western liberals and strengthened the desire for a National Home where the Jews could build a new state and live without fear. The tragedy was that they could only achieve this through the use of the same weapons which so often in the past had been used against them — terror and force.

The indigenous Palestinian Arabs had lived side by side with Jews for centuries in peace and mutual tolerance. But with the influx of the European Jews of a radically different way of life, imbued with aggressive nationalism, and with their terrorist organizations, the Arabs reacted by forming a resistance. Consequently, during the British mandate, strikes and demonstrations were common in Palestine, until the colonial administration broke down altogether and the problem was handed over to the United Nations. The United Nations was faced with a vastly changed situation from that of 1919, for since that time large numbers of Jews had migrated from Europe. On 29th November 1947, a settlement was recommended which created a Jewish State and gave 56% of Palestine to the Jews, 43% to the Arabs and declared an international zone including Jerusalem and its environs on the remaining 1%. The fighting which broke out in 1948 resulted in the Jews occupying 77% of Palestine. Effectively Palestine had disappeared from the political map. But its people could not disappear and they remained either in huge refugee camps or became political exiles in other Arab countries. The freedom of political expression, the right of self-government, and the civil and personal liberties achieved by the Jews were taken away from the Palestinians. They left their homes, land and possessions behind them in Israel.

It is a sad irony that liberty for one means a loss of liberty for another. Since the deprivation of the Palestinians, the struggle against the state of Israel and Zionism has continued. It will continue, not because of the support given to it by other Arab nations and the Soviet Union or because

Israel has taken more and more territory through her con-
quests, or because of an unfavourable international situation, but because a whole people have been unjustly depriv-
ed of their basic freedoms. It is the belief of the writer that
justice is indivisible and that what is justice for the Jews
must also be justice for the Palestinians.

"Palestinian Exiles," *The Times*, London (February 18, 1972).

Sir, Your sympathetic coverage of the immigration of the Russian Jews to Israel encourages me to write to you about a comparable issue.

As a Palestinian who has been in England since early 1966 and whose aged parents have been displaced as a result of the 1967 June War, I approached the Israeli consulate in London requesting that my parents be allowed to return and "spend the last days of their lives at their home in Jericho." After approximately four months of futile correspondence with the Israeli authorities, I offered to go back myself to Jericho with the sole purpose of facilitating the filling in of the necessary application forms, etc, which would enable my parents to return on the grounds of "family reunification." This request has also been rejected.

My parents' case is, of course, not an isolated one. There are thousands of Palestinians who are enduring acute hardships in refugee camps surrounding the Jordan Valley, often within sight of their homes, and who are longing to return.

I am hopeful that those of your readers who are campaigning for the "ingathering of the exiles" will remember that the Palestinians' exodus is still within living memory and that the Palestinians will continue to refuse to settle anywhere else in view of the fact that Palestine is the rightful home of their ancient heritage and culture.

London

"How the Middle East Ceasefire Should Be Made to Work," *The Guardian*, London (October 24, 1973).

Sir, The acceptance of a ceasefire by Egypt and Israel may or may not lead eventually to a permanent settlement of the Middle East conflict. What is definite, however, is that this latest flare-up in the Middle East will have clearly claimed a heavy toll of life on both sides. Israel's legendary invincibility has been broken, and that myth will never be restored—now is the time for an urgent and sober reassessment of the place of Israel by Jewish leaders all over the world.

Does Israel as a Zionist state have any future? As architects and proponents of the policies which finally left the Arabs with no choice but to fight, Mrs. Meir and her Government are accountable to the international community, particularly the Jews, for the massive loss of life sustained in this latest conflict. Zionism is clearly incapable of achieving its claimed objectives—on the contrary, it is leading the Israelis into a dead and dangerous end. Israel is beset by socio-economic contradictions and is a society with no deep-rooted past. In peacetime, these factors, combined with Israel's almost total dependence on foreign aid, constitute a grave threat to the internal stability of the country. In war, the loss of one battle to the Arabs would inevitably lead to the destruction of Israel as a state.

In view of this, no matter what the final outcome of this

particular war, it is to the future that we must look, and here only an Israel which is an integral part of the Arab world has a place.

Oxford

"Britain and the Middle East," *The Times*, London (December 23, 1974).

Sir, Your favourable comments about the Jewish people in general, and the Israelis in particular (*The Times* leader, December 14), would be more honourable if they were not made at the expense of the Palestinians. It is difficult to see how anyone taking an objective view of the Middle East conflict could deny that it is we, the Palestinians, who have on balance suffered the greater injustice.

The fact that you so frankly state that you do not subscribe to this school of thought can only be explained by the fact that the Israelis, as your leader states, are a people for whom you have a special regard, just as you do for the French, whereas by implication the Palestinians are not, and an infringement of the political and civil rights of the Palestinians is presumably therefore neither here nor there. Thus you defend *The Times* against the unjustified accusation that it accepted an advertisement which might instigate racial hatred by presenting a defence which itself gives the Palestinians as strong a case as any for feeling run down on racial grounds.

The Palestinian Arabs, sir, are no barbarians. They are a civilized people whose ancestors carried the torch of civilization long before Europe evolved its now commendable and noble values. Paradoxically our contacts with Europe, first with the Crusades, then with the British man-

16

date and then, as a result, with the Zionist movement, have hardly contributed to our cherished standards of morality.

Since the invasion of our homeland by the Zionist movement we have been steadily pushed into committing acts which we would have previously unequivocally condemned. For in Palestine, the Jewish people, often great makers of history, have refused to learn their lesson from it, and have accepted to apply persecution in its crudest forms against the Palestinians. The true friends of the Jewish people would be those who had the courage to tell them that Zionism is wrong, very wrong, and that now is the time for abandoning it.

Beirut

"Iraq—No Bitterness before the Provocations of Zionism," *The Guardian*, London (September 12, 1975).*

Sir, In a confidential despatch to the Foreign Office which is dated December 1934, this is how Sir F. Humphrys, the then-British Ambassador in Baghdad, described the position of the Jewish community in Iraq. "Before the war they probably enjoyed a more favourable position than any other minority in the country. Since 1920, however, Zionism has sown dissension between Jews and Arabs, and a bitterness has grown up between the two peoples which did not previously exist. . . .The wiser and more experienced Jews, while probably sympathising with the general aims of the Zionist movement, openly deplore the unfortunate repercussions which it has had on their position in Iraq.

"They appreciate that feeling is only exacerbated by Zionist propaganda, and they have no desire that it should be extended in this country. . . .Jewish newspapers, both British and Palestinian, frequently contain scurrilous attacks on the Iraqi Government, and grossly misleading accounts of the situation of the Jews in this country. . . . In these circumstances it is, I think, understandable that the

---

*Editor's note: In the summer of 1975 the Iraqi government placed a number of advertisements in some Western newspapers inviting those Iraqi Jews who had fled the country after 1948 to return home. These advertisements were met by fierce criticism from Zionist leaders and spokesmen, and the newspapers in which they appeared were subjected to all kinds of denunciations.

authorities should tend to strike at the roots of the trouble by endeavouring to prevent the circulation of publications containing provocative attacks on Iraq.

"Indeed, there is much to be said for the banning of such literature in the interests of the Jews themselves, since the exacerbation of feeling which follows its entry into this country seriously impairs their relations with the Arabs. . . . In my view, there is no natural antagonism between Jews and Arabs in Iraq. . . . Normally the two communities are friendly towards each other." (Eastern, E 7707/6495/93).

May I end by assuring you that no Palestinian I know would subject your paper to any form of abuse were you to accept an advertisement from the Israeli embassy inviting the Palestinians to return home.

Oxford

"The Accusation of Racialism against Zionism," *The Times*, London (November 22, 1975).

Sir, During a visit to this university by Mr. Abba Eban three years ago, I asked him simply to inform an audience of over 500 people why he, a South African, had *more* right than me, a Palestinian, to live and settle in Palestine. In characteristic fashion, Mr. Eban's lengthy reply never actually answered that question.

Now that he is no longer a member of the Israeli Cabinet, I hope that you will allow me the courtesy of your columns to put yet another simple question to Mr. Eban, in the hope that he will feel able to be more forthcoming.

Could he, or perhaps any of your readers, tell me why is it that even that handful of non-Jewish communities in Israel, such as the Druze, who have *accepted* the Zionist ideology, do not and cannot enjoy full political and civil rights?

Oxford

"Israel's Dream and Reality," *The Guardian*, London (March 3, 1976).

Sir, May I be allowed to add the following comments to your thoughtful leader "Misfortunes of Mr. Rabin"?

The significant difference between the pre-Rabin era and the present lies not so much in any qualitative change in the Israeli leadership as in the final realization by important sectors of the world community of the many fundamental shortcomings of Zionism, and of the urgent neglected problem of the Palestinian people. Israel's mounting difficulties are therefore to be explained not so much in terms of the greater "glamour, stature, and vision" of the earlier "rules of the game" as by the fact that the "game" itself has, as was inevitable, changed profoundly.

Former Israeli leaders conveniently disregarded the Palestinians as the main factor in their conflict with the Arabs. Thus among earlier "visionary" leaders the late Ben Gurion, a gifted linguist, never even saw the necessity of learning Arabic, and throughout her term of office, Golda Meir openly declared that the Palestinians did not exist.

Now that the Palestinians have at last acquired a relatively more favourable position in the international arena, any Israeli leader would be ill-advised to continue ignoring their problem. However, recent reports seem to suggest that the Israeli government, possibly with the tacit approval of certain Arab governments, is now seeking the setting of an administratively autonomous entity on the West Bank.

Should these speculations prove true, they would be further evidence of the Israelis' strange understanding of the dynamics of social and political change now at work in the Middle East. In this sense at least, Mr. Rabin's government is no different from any of its predecessors. And here I see no reason why this attitude will not continue as long as Zionism, and not only the individual personalities in charge, is not brought into question. For while as a "dream" Zionism may have succeeded in transferring substantial numbers of world Jewry to the "land of milk and honey," as a political doctrine it must now face the facts and turn its attention to the aspirations and interests of the Palestinian people, whose roots in that land are no vision, but painfully real.

Oxford

"Arab Uses of Wealth," *The Times*, London (July 6, 1976).

Sir, The reported attempt of some Arab businessmen to buy the site of the battle of Hastings fills me with dismay. It reflects ignorance and insensitivity of the first order, and I am certain that the overwhelming majority of thinking Arabs would view it with the contempt it deserves, just as they would had the purchaser been an American or Japanese businessman bidding to acquire the site of the battle of al-Qadisiya or al-Yarmuk.

It is not as if the Arab world had reached the level of development which might make such excursions of fantasies at best amusing. Unhappily, despite the creditable progress the Arabs have made on the path towards social and economic development, many parts of the Arab world are still desperately lacking in the most basic provisions of modern life.

My body aches every time I think of a dangerously bumpy ride I managed to endure on the major road from Damascus to Jordan over a year ago. The main road connecting Jordan and Iraq, over which economically vital commercial traffic to the Arabian Gulf must pass, is even worse. Nor is it a credit to certain Arab countries that many of their people still fly out to remote lands merely to treat as basic a complaint as tonsillitis.

Similarly, although virtually every Arab child can now have a free education, the general standard, particularly at a higher level, leaves much to be desired. Apart from having to cope with appalling crowdedness, most Arab universities, crippled by lack of resources and efficient administration, find themselves forced to keep surgery hours (many are closed by 1 pm and not always as a result of the dictates of the climate).

It is perhaps ironical that despite all the wealth with which some Arab states have been endowed, there is nowhere in the Arab world an independent scholarship fund to which promising Arab scholars could turn for the support of their education. In most parts of the Arab world, apart from the exceptionally affluent regions where scholarships for nationals can be had for the asking, there is absolutely no way for a needy and independent student, short of selling his soul to the ruling regime or charming a top civil servant, to pursue his studies without falling hopelessly in debt. Completely forgotten, it seems, is the Arab tradition of fostering learning, when writers and scientists used to be rewarded with their work's weight in gold.

It is such serious shortcomings which lead me to believe that the present boom in some parts of the Arab world is an ailment not disimilar to a tumour. The apparent lack of efficient and long-term planning may well lead the Arabs, once the wealth of oil has inevitably evaporated, back into poverty and their luxury abodes into delapidation.

Then the struggle for economic survival will need other battle grounds than those of Hastings.

Oxford

"Hijack Leader," *The Guardian,* **London (July 16, 1976).**

Sir, The obvious moral which the Palestinians are likely to draw from the overall reaction in the West to the Entebbe episode is that, in politics, almost any action can be justified by its success.

Oxford

Unpublished Letter to the Editor, *The Times*, London (April 24, 1979).

Dear Sir, The recent signing of an Israeli-Egyptian "Peace" Treaty is a depressing testimony to the fact that war remains an ever-effective instrument of diplomacy. For in the final analysis, it is the benefits of the 1967 war which the Israelis are now reaping from a tamed Egypt.

Egypt, a pioneer of Arab nationalism, a vigorous promoter of its culture and jealous guardian of its destiny, was a natural opponent of the emergence of Zionism. Its sacrifices for Arab causes and its positive participation in struggles for independence cannot be exaggerated.

Nevertheless, there are two sides to the balance sheet of Egypt's involvement in Arab politics. Whereas its support has given Arab causes a considerable leverage, its identification with them developed into a fertile source from which Egypt itself drew considerable political and economic powers. For the Israelis, on the other hand, Egypt constituted the most formidable and credible opponent on the Arab side, an opponent whose military strength could grow to seriously challenge, perhaps overwhelm, that of their own. The neutralization of Egypt therefore has always been one of Israel's most cherished aims. But Egypt's commitment to the Palestinian cause was unequivocal. It is common knowledge that, when Egypt was engaged in wars with the Israelis, the question of control over the Sinai desert was in no way at the centre of the Israeli-Arab conflict.

Egypt went to war, or, more precisely, was dragged into it, because, like its sister Arab States, it opposed Zionism and rightly viewed it as a colonialist movement which made no secret of its intention to create in an already populated and flourishing Arab Palestine, an exclusively Jewish State as "Jewish as England was English."

Of course, even the most cynical of Palestinians might not go as far as to say that Egypt has now accepted this eventuality; indeed, there are those amongst us who believe that many Egyptians do not support Sadat's policies, even as far as they went. But the point is that the Israeli-Palestinian conflict would have existed, and shall continue to exist, whether or not Egypt, alone or in conjunction with other Arab States, accepted an Israel which continued to disregard the national rights of the Palestinians, pretending that they did not exist, and adhering to its aim of reincarnating Zion.

The simple reality is that four million Palestinians (not only the one million living in the West Bank) will refuse to wither away. They are alive and well. Those Palestinians are among the most educated people in the Middle East, including Israel. Amongst them, there are artists, scientists, scholars, nuns, nurses, sportsmen, lawyers, moderates, extremists, Christians, Muslims, agnostics — in short, all the diverse elements of a modern society. The tragedy of what has befallen them must be depressingly familiar to the majority of readers. Nevertheless, it is to their perception of the Zionist movement that the new "prophets" of peace must turn if they were to realize the genuine peace they claim to seek and which the peoples of the area, not to say the world, need so much. To us Palestinians, the Zionists did not come to Palestine to preach peace, and this is why, so long as they adhere to their Zionist ideology, we would be hard put to believe in their sincerity in seeking a peaceful solution to the problems they have created.

Even after the emergence of the State of Israel in 1948, the Zionist aim of colonizing all of Palestine, indeed all of the ancient fertile crescent, was *never renounced*. It is in this context that the final occupation of the West Bank and the systematic destruction of the Palestinian nation, sometimes literally, should be seen. So long as Israel adhered to the fundamental principles of Zionism, the threat to the Palestinian people remained all too conclusive. Even as recently as the early seventies, we find Zionist leaders, such as Moshe Dayan, advocating what amounts to a "final solution" of the Palestinian problem, namely that Israel would have preferred to have the land (in this case, the West Bank) without the people.

It should therefore be clear from this that peace in the Middle East will not be realized by Israel's adjusting its frontiers with this or that sovereign state, but by revising the basic philosophy underlying its policies with those most adversely affected by them, the Palestinians. This would naturally require a majority of Israelis to follow the steps of what some of them already do and advocate, namely the re-examination of Zionism itself and the acceptance of the facts that Zionist ideology is anachronistic, that justice is indivisible and that what is justice for the Jews must also be justice for the Palestinians. Unhappily for all concerned, however, no such fundamental changes in Zionist attitudes appear to be in sight, and it seems that Zionism, this hypnotic creature, will continue to be fed regardless.

Paris

"An Obstacle Course to Peace in the Middle East," *The New York Times* (June 4, 1980).

To the Editor:

It is by a twist of logic that Dov Ronen [Op-Ed May 2] complains that no responsible Palestinian has given emphatic assurances concerning the future security of Israel. This demand is as valid as that of a surgeon prompting a patient who is about to have his legs amputated to undertake never to participate in a marathon race after the operation.

Indeed, Israeli generals themselves are in the habit of boasting about the potency of their army and how relatively feeble the combined forces of the Arab States are.

So Mr. Ronen's fears cannot be taken seriously. Instead, as someone of obviously high intellect, benefiting from one of the world's most privileged intellectual environments, one would have expected Mr. Ronen to look at the more profound obstacles standing in the way of peaceful settlement of this tragic conflict.

It would be hard for anyone taking an objective stand on the Middle East problem not to attribute the Israeli-Arab conflict to the very fundamentals of Zionism, which is still adhered to, almost to the letter, by the present ruling elite in Israel. I say elite rather than government because in the final analysis all of those who governed Israel, right from its emergence as a state, never really deviated from that colonialist doctrine.

Therefore, at a time when one Israeli Government follows another in passing recommendations for more Israeli settlements on occupied Arab territory and for more expropriation of Palestinian land, it is futile to refer to Palestinians' lack of conciliation as a reason for the grounding of the peace process.

Both in human and in material terms, the Palestinian Arabs have paid an unbearably high price as a result of Israel's creation. Mr. Ronen writes movingly of having lost most of his school friends in the aftermath of the Holocaust, though I am sure that in no way would he lay the blame for that shameful episode of European history on us Palestinians. Nevertheless, we Palestinians have also had our holocaust. I, too, have lost many of my school friends and many other friends of my youth.

Given the unspeakable sufferings of the Palestinians, and the gigantic proportions of their losses, it is really remarkable to take them to task for refusing to renounce one of the few symbols of their determination. Which other resistance group has compromised its "maximalist" aims while in opposition?

It is an empirically established fact that the responsibilities of office do temper even the most intransigent of leaders (with the possible exception of Israel), and should the Palestinians be finally offered the state they rightly claim, they would have little incentive to continue the cycle of violence which has claimed so many innocent lives and led to the breaking up of so many homes.

Paris

"Synagogue Bombing," *The International Herald Tribune*, Paris (October 16, 1980).

Sir, It is curious that you chose to publish a speculative report implicating an Arab in the recent bombing of a synagogue in Paris (IHT, Oct. 10).

In addition to the fact that such an act of violence is objectively abhorrent, the Palestinian Arabs have added reasons to view it for the horror it is. For it is the Palestinians who are still paying a high price for the atrocities of Nazism in Europe, which gave momentum to the cause of Zionism. Even for reasons of expediency, it is hardly plausible for the Palestinians to sponsor an act which would surely undermine their relations with a country which is showing an increasing understanding of their plight.

It would be more intelligent to keep at least two points in mind when speculating about the authors of this recent tragic incident.

First of all, the Jewish community in France is far from being united and there are French Jews who view with discontent what they consider to be the community's failure to identify completely with Zionists' interests.

Secondly, the Zionist movement has in the past shown its readiness to go to any limits in demonstrating the supposed impossibility for Jews to assimilate in Gentile societies, even to the extent of turning its guns against its co-religionists. The most dramatic instance was the bombing of a Jewish synagogue in Baghdad in 1951 by Israeli agents.

Paris

"The Arab World Revisited," *Le Monde* (November 18, 1980).

PARIS — My Dear Conscience, as you can see, I have finally succumbed to your persistence, packed up my belongings and travelled back to our Arab world. It is only right for me to tell you how different it is from what you told me it was.

Let me say at once that I speak as a great believer in our People's resourcefulness and ultimate wisdom, but even at the risk of being dismissed as petty-minded, can you at least understand my disillusion when I walk the length of a main boulevard of an Arab capital and do not find a public place where I could wash my hands? In the meantime, development projects are planned and executed at breathtaking speed, but in many cases in areas where they would only be inhabited by ghosts, once the momentary causes of wealth evaporate, as they inevitably will. Of course I am not telling you about the impressive increase in literacy rate, nor the apparent improvement of Public Health, nor the imaginative agricultural projects which are turning hitherto barren land into green pastures.

I am not telling all of that because I think that such progress is expected from a People whose ancestors have made striking contributions to the civilization of Mankind. But expected or not, these pockets of progress are not matched by an intellectual renaissance. While man for man I have come across some individuals who can rightly claim high standards of intelligence and cultural finesse, it is a fact that their noble qualities can scarcely be attributed to most of the systems engulfing them. Students are still rounded up in some Arab universities for expressing their genuine and completely justified grievances, and Arab prisons are not empty of men whose only crime is to speak or write against the governing elite.

Saddest of all, even political formations which were heralded some years ago as the bearers of the torch of progressive change are manifesting similar patterns of behavior, and their attitude of raising the best-connected rather than the best-qualified has inevitably deflated the enthusiasm with which they were initially greeted by the Arab intelligentsia.

Worst of all, the Arab world has hardly ever been more disunited. You must have heard of Mansour, a member of the Bath party, who was killed by Farouk, another member of the Bath party, in the name of Arab unity!

You say that ours is an area undergoing significant social and economic changes and that what I am protesting against is not more than the pain of growth. Of course there is some truth in this. But at least some of this pain could be avoided had it not been for the fact that many of our rulers behave as if they had a divine right to rule. You cannot be a skeptic in this land. If you are not with the ruler then you are automatically against him and may God have mercy on you. It might have been tolerable if these rulers were not accumulating fortunes enough to give them and their descendants many times their needs and for centuries to come.

The other day I read a report about an Arab shaikh who had twenty million dollars worth of jewelry stolen from his Cannes apartment. Can you imagine how many of our children could have been educated with this? Do you remember our having to work on the motorway in order to pay our fees at Oxford? What happened to your oil wells, you Arabs? Our workmates never stopped asking.

You are never tired of saying that one day the Arabs will stop providing Israel with its main source of strength and that they will somehow fold up their petty quarrels and channel their potential strength towards redressing one of the gravest injustices of modern history. I myself started to share your optimism after Israel's declaration [on July 31, 1980] of Jerusalem as its eternal capital. Now, I said, the Israelis have really gone far too far. Even some of my Western friends reacted to the news with indignation and visible grief. The Arab response was bound to be firm and decisive.

By now you know that that black day of Arab history turned out like any other day—business as usual; Arab radios and televisions continued to blurt out their melancholic songs of love, and while Arab armies dug in deeper on the frontiers of their Arab neighbors, their leaders issued their ritual communiques condemning the flagrant Israeli intrusion on the sacred rights of the Arabs. And so Jerusalem was the latest prey to be devoured by the Israeli fact-creating monster. Can you really blame me for finding our World so stifling, so small?

Once again I take the road, though with a heavy heart, a measure of hope, and a determination never to forget.

"We the Palestinians," *Le Monde* (Tuesday, June 22, 1982).

PARIS—It might appear redundant to assert a people's right to live. But doesn't the devastation of Lebanon and the killing of tens of civilians by the regular Israeli army justify such a discourse?

We Palestinians are human beings and we have a fundamental right to live. We did not choose the circumstances of our birth any more than you did. Left alone, we would have chosen to stay in the homes and farms of our ancestors. Instead, we found ourselves unwanted strangers in our own homeland, constantly being chased, with no right to protest or to exercise our basic rights as citizens.

In spite of this hostile environment many of us managed to survive. Being a people not lacking in history or cultural heritage, we have continued to claim a place in modern world society. Our youth now has a presence in most professions. Amongst us, there are poets, engineers, workers, peasants, artists, doctors, nurses and all other elements of modern society. When we are not working, we long for and, when we can, take refuge in the same sorts of distractions you might indulge in. A Palestinian youth might spend his free time listening to or playing a tune, watching or playing a match of tennis, reading or writing, passing hours bavarding in the local cafe. Altogether there is nothing so extraordinary about him. The main charac-

39

teristic which might distinguish him from you, or the man next door to you, is the fact of his nationality. For being Palestinian, in the modern sense, signifies a belonging to a species which is like the Jews of the Third Reich, becoming incessantly threatened with extinction.

Since the immigration of Zionist Jews to Palestine during the turn of this century, followed by the creation of the state of Israel in 1948, nearly one tenth of the Palestinian population has perished under an Israeli reign of terror. Once the counting of the victims of the latest genocide is over, this figure will become old news.

To some, the deaths of Palestinian and Lebanese civilians in Lebanon might have little more than a statistical significance, just as the torture of Iranian liberals under the late Shah was viewed with such indifference that the unhappy country was driven into a wave of hysteria against the Shah's former allies. At least an important part of what is happening in Iran today is due to the West's lack of vision. In the Arab world, it is possible to foresee a time when the moderation of Yasser Arafat or the academic rationality of Georges Habash will be recalled with nostalgia. Amongst the Arab masses, the classical situation of a role looking for a hero does now exist. This hero will be born out of the stifling frustrations being felt by those masses. He will be urged to throw over the wall all the conventions which his people are being asked to respect, and which the Israelis are being tolerated for violating. He will be expected to sentence the oil wells to fire, and in the smoke of the aftermath to work on inciting popular uprisings against those regimes desperately lacking in legitimacy. He will call for

Albanising the Arab countries to the outside world. All of this might not be so far away if the West does not take decisive steps to control Israel, this Frankenstein they have created. Left to their own devices and with the army at their disposal, Menachem Begin and his followers will continue to pose a serious threat to world peace. It is not a day too early for the West to take concrete action to contain the terrifying fanaticism of these men and to forestall the tragic eventuality of their terrorist practices. The West will have to go beyond expressing verbal sympathy for the Palestinian people while at the same time pouring unlimited money and arms into Israel.

If I am appealing to the West it is because the West cannot wash its hands of the responsibility for the prolonged sufferings of the Palestinians which resulted from the creation of a Jewish state in Palestine. To whom else can I appeal? To the Arab governments? Every Palestinian must now be questioning his belonging to the Arab world. It is superfluous to say that the hegemony of Zionism was a threat to all Arabs, not only to the Palestinians, and that our struggle went hand in hand with that of Arab nationalist movements fighting for their independence and liberty.

Furthermore, even in the diaspora, we have played a significant role in the building of the cultural and economic infrastructure of many Arab countries, especially those of the Gulf.

Nevertheless, we are convinced that the march of history will pull the Arab giant out of its hypnotic sleep and that the winds of change will awaken the Arab conscience to its historic responsibilities.

As to the Palestinian resistance, it will not disappear. They might kill our leaders or massacre our fighters, but the Israelis should know that no one can ever exterminate a people.

"Reply to Kissinger," *The International Herald Tribune,* Paris (Saturday-Sunday, July 3-4, 1982).

Sir, (Regarding "Kissinger on Lebanon, the West Bank, the Gulf," *The International Herald Tribune,* June 17) Henry Kissinger would do humanity a service by drifting from the stage of international politics into oblivion. He is certainly not qualified to talk about the tragic events in Lebanon, for which he must bear at least part of the responsibility.

His shuttle diplomacy concentrated more on excluding the Soviet Union from the Geneva conference than on finding an urgent peaceful settlement for the Arab-Israeli conflict. It culminated in the severing of Egypt from the Arab world and thus sowed further dissension in an area so needy of stability. This added fragmentation of the Arab world must have considerably encouraged Israel to unleash its campaign of terror.

Henry Kissinger qualifies the general position of the Reagan administration on the Lebanese holocaust as wise and statesmanlike. Yet it should be clear to all thinking people that Israel has already done colossal, perhaps irreparable damage to American interests in the Middle East.

Although created and nourished by the West, Israel has grown into a Frankenstein which is turning against its master. Does the West have to wait for the rise of an Arab Khomeini before grasping this basic point?

Even as far as strictly Israeli interests are concerned, time will show that Israel's leaders have undermined all possibilities for coexistence between their people and the Palestinians. Of course, the Palestinians might lose this battle and the next, but what fire does not destroy, it hardens. They will come back, stronger and more determined to continue their national struggle for freedom and liberty.

Given the recent massacres of Palestinian and Lebanese civilians, "if I were an Israeli parent," as Peter Calvocoressi wrote recently in The Sunday Times, "I would tremble for my children and my children's children."

Paris

"Let's Save Israel from Herself," *Le Monde* (Tuesday, August 17, 1982).

PARIS — Is there a symbiotic relationship between the Jewish psyche and persecution? The tragic episode of Jewish persecution by European fascists is barely over. Yet, the victims of yesterday's holocaust are already setting the scene for a second act of persecution against themselves. It is all the more ironic that they are doing so in a region where they have found one of the safest havens of their history. It will be astonishing if the Arabs will ever forget the crimes being committed against their brethren in the name of the future of the Jewish people. Not long ago, I was a sincere believer in the PLO's declared aim of working towards the creation of a secular democratic state in Palestine where Palestinian Arabs and Israeli Jews could live together in harmony. Now I do not even dare discuss this noble concept with many of my fellow Palestinians. The Israeli campaign of terror against the Lebanese and Palestinians has created so much animosity that it is already hard to imagine a day when the Palestinian and Israeli people could co-exist. In addition to human and material casualties, this vision of the future has also fallen victim to the rain of bombs and bullets.

The Israelis must surely know that they have no future

in the Arab World except as a Middle Eastern state. They cannot continue being a western outpost sustained by a favourable balance of force. It is a matter of time before the Arabs master the techniques of modern warfare. The Arabs' state of apparent stoicism will not last forever; sooner or later more nationalist regimes will emerge in the area, and the Arabs may finally succeed in unifying their ranks. To the Israelis the outcome of such an eventuality should be obvious. To win the goodwill and acceptance of the Arabs therefore should be an essential part of Israel's strategy for survival. Instead the Israelis are pursuing a policy which is turning them into the principal architects of their own future destruction. Out of the ruins of Beirut, the Palestine Liberation Organization will emerge as the vanguard of a vaster and more radical Arab Liberation Organization.

The history of the region provides ample precedents for military setbacks sparking off revolt. The most dramatic example is the rise of Nasserism to its apogee after the military defeat of Nasser in 1956. It is surely no accident that shortly afterwards the Middle East was plunged into a period of radicalisation with the overthrow of the monarchy in Iraq, an attempted coup d'etat in Jordan, a civil war in Lebanon, the deposing of King Saud, the rise of the republicans in Yemen and, of course, the union between Syria and Egypt. Should Begin and Sharon push their "infernal logic" against the PLO and Lebanon to its disastrous conclusions, the Arab world will erupt with the violence of a volcano and the region will become an unsafe place for the Jews and their allies for decades to come.

This will be partly as an immediate reaction to Israel's military adventures, but also as a long-overdue response to the intrinsic aggression of Zionism. Fundamentally, Zionism is a colonialist ideology which feeds on the tension it creates between Jews and Palestinians. It is oppressive if only in the simple fact that it called for the creation of an exclusively Jewish State in an already populated land. Thus, the cold logic of Zionism dictates that the indigenous people of the coveted land had to be either expelled, destroyed, or at best oppressed. As far as expulsion goes, the Palestinian exodus is too well known to need emphasising. Begin and Sharon make no effort to hide their intention of making this exodus as total and irreversible as possible. It is they who are advocating the creation of a Palestinian State on a land that does not belong to the Palestinians, namely Jordan, overlooking the paradox of inflicting on the Jordanians what the Israelis have inflicted on the Palestinians.

As for destruction, Israeli leaders are open about their aim of eliminating the PLO, although one way or another the PLO embraces all Palestinians within its infrastructure of schools, hospitals, research centres and industries.

Finally, as for oppression, even the most cynical observer would admit that those Palestinians living under Israeli law, be it in Israel proper or in the occupied territories, are subjected to the crudest forms of discrimination and oppression. It is enough to remember that at a time when the European Human Rights Commission has recommended the prohibition of the use of rubber bullets in dispersing demonstrations, the Israeli army have killed Palestinian demonstrators in the West Bank with real bullets.

These three morbid options of expelling, destroying or oppressing the Palestinian people are the mathematical conclusions of the Zionist equation. By articulating the national aspirations of the Palestinians, and by taking up arms to defend their cause, the PLO has posed a serious challenge to the basic principles of Zionism. What is remarkable is that, in their euphoria, Zionists are forgetting the fact that it is they who have unwittingly created the PLO, and that as long as Zionism remains what it is, there will always be a PLO determined to fight to redress one of the greatest injustices of modern history.

It is painful to us Palestinians to hear people say that while they feel sympathy for our plight, we should understand that the Jews have a biblical right to Palestine, as if what happened to us is the will of God, as if God participates in the macabre dance of politics.

Whatever the validity of this, the creation of Israel has inflicted on the Palestinians an overwhelming injustice. The PLO's resort to armed struggle is merely a means of redress. It would renounce its fight the day overdue justice is brought to the Palestinians. In fact, for the last ten years, leaders of the PLO have been concentrating more on finding a diplomatic solution to the Palestinian problem. Arafat's signing of a document accepting all U.N. resolutions on the Palestinian question is but the latest evidence of these efforts. Israel's reaction to Arafat's overtures was predictable and is consistent with the dictates of Zionism. As Zionists, the Israeli ruling elite cannot accept any idea which does not lead to the expulsion, destruction, or oppression of the Palestinians. The most striking example of this is the reaction of the Israeli Ambassador to Paris:* "We will only negotiate with the elected representatives of the Palestinians on the West Bank." What the Ambassador forgot to add is that Israel has been systematically dismissing the elected representatives of the Palestinians on the West Bank and that, subsequent to Israel's creation, three million out of the four million Palestinians have been forced into the disapora. Perhaps the Ambassador hopes that by the end of the present war, there will be no Palestinians left except those living on the West Bank!

Is there a way out of this total impasse? The only realistic hope which can spare our two peoples further bloodshed and prevent the smouldering anger of the Arabs bursting into flames is for the U.S. to *impose* a just settlement on the region. To achieve this, they should not commit the grave mistake of incarnating such old and futile approaches as Kissinger's shuttle diplomacy. What is needed now are daring new ideas unhindered by influence, whatever its source. Here their European allies, who have experience and deep traditional links with the Arab world, could play a significant role. In so doing, not only will the U.S. serve its long term interests in the area, but may also succeed in saving Israel from itself.

---

*Editor's note: Moshe Arens, now Israeli Minister without Portfolio.

"The Warnings that the World Would Not Heed," *The Observer*, London (Sunday, September 26, 1982).

PARIS—Today, while Palestinians everywhere weep in silent rage, they wish that they had been spared the empty gratification of having their worst fears about Zionism confirmed. For more than 40 years they have appealed to mankind to forestall the inevitable threat which Zionism posed to their existence. But, like Caesar before the Ides of March, the world heeded none of their warnings.

What happened in the refugee camps of Beirut last Black Friday is only the culmination of what has been happening to the Palestinian people for four decades.

Only in the number of victims do the Sabra and Chatila massacres differ from the tragic litany of those earlier nightmares of Deir Yassin, Kalonia, Qibya, Kafr Qasim, Qalqilya, Nabi Elian, Azzun, Khan Youis and Sammu. In April 1948, while the Palestinian village of Deir Yassin on the outskirts of Jerusalem slept, armed members of the Zionist underground gang Irgun attacked, butchering 243 men, women and children in a raid which even most Jews disowned. Their leader was none other than Menachem Begin, now Prime Minister of Israel.

Five years later, a similar raid on the unsuspecting inhabitants of Qibya, which left 75 slaughtered, was led by General Ariel Sharon, now the man who controls the reins of Israel's Army. We Palestinians cried out against these crimes, the United Nations confirmed our "claims," but the world was too busy washing its conscience of the stains from the Second World War crimes committed against the Jews to listen to our unpleasant bulletins.

Now that, thanks to on-the-spot reporting, a population is being exterminated in full newsreel colour under your very nose, will you continue to look the other way? Will you, once more, join the chorus singing yet another Zionist hymn: that this mass murder was committed only by the troops of Major Sa'ad Haddad (which are none other than the "Lebanese Brigade" of the Israeli Army), and that the regular units of the scrupulously vigilant Israeli Armed Forces had nothing to do with it?

Is not this cowardly, hideous massacre — the cold-blooded murder of Palestinians, young and old, babies and adolescents, men and women, Muslims and Christians — consistent with the logic of a Zionism which, in its endeavour to establish an Israel "as Jewish as England is English" in our homeland, has sought our destruction, our expulsion, or at best, our oppression?

You refused to read the writing on the wall. How can the world absolve itself from the responsibility for what has already befallen us, and for what is befalling us now? We, the Palestinians, have been crying danger from our mosques and churches, from the playgrounds of our schools and the courtyards of our homes, and even — when in your more reflective moods you allowed it — from the airwaves of your radio and television stations.

Our story is too obvious to have been misunderstood. Very

simply, we are a people, we have been robbed of our homeland, and all the sophistry of the world will not make us accept this as our destiny.

In its implacable campaign against us, Zionist propaganda stopped at nothing to deprive us of what was ours. It distorted our stature: in its literature, we, the descendants of the forefathers of civilization, were reduced to scattered bedouins aimlessly roaming the desert. It obliterated our history: Palestine, the most ancient country, ceased to exist in their made-to-measure historical narratives, which were swallowed whole by the media.

Thinking people everywhere should have known better: the world's ancient travellers and artists had told and shown otherwise. Yet many of you filled your ears with cotton wool and placed blindfolds upon your eyes, preferring not to know—and so in spite of the inherent dangers of Zionism, Israel was planted as a Western outpost in our midst.

Justifying the invasion of West Beirut, the Israeli Ambassador to Paris* declared last week: "In the Orient there is blood vengeance." Presumably he meant that the non-Oriental, and therefore civilized and humane, Israeli Army went into the city in order to protect its sworn enemies, the Palestinians, the Progressives, the anti-Phalangist Christians, etc., against vengeance from their adversaries. His comment is all the more incredible coming from a spokesman for a State which has just exacted thousands of eyes for an eye. Is revenge, then, the monopoly of Orientals? In any case, to which camp does Israel belong? Is it only oriental in the position it has staked out on the map?

---

*Editor's note: Moshe Arens, now Israeli Minister without Portfolio.

Once, some of us believed co-existence was possible with Israel. Now, when the final body count is being totalled from last week's horror at the camps of Sabra and Chatila, let it not be forgotten that the slim hope for co-existence between Palestinians and Israelis had fallen there as well, not the least of its victims.

Should anyone therefore be astonished now if, in our rage and despair, there is a revival of Palestinian extremism — a call for the Israelis to get out and never return, ever?

"What Are the Palestinian People Supposed to Feel Now?" *The International Herald Tribune*, Paris (Tuesday, September 28, 1982).

PARIS — How many massacres, how many more men and women, babies and adolescents, Christians and Moslems, how many more Jews and Palestinians must die before the world awakes from its torpor, regains its senses and finds the courage to say what we Palestinians have said all along: that the orthodox Zionism religiously adhered to by Israel's rulers is a disastrous doctrine for us as well as for the Jews?

How could it be otherwise? How could the world have been duped into believing that this anachronistic ideology could ever succeed in creating a Jewish state in an already populated land, without bloody conflict?

Was it apathy? Perhaps. But the main reason was understandably that, after the horrors of World War II, the world was too busy scrubbing away the stains of shame from its recent history, not knowing meanwhile — not wanting to know — that another episode of human tragedy was systematically in progress elsewhere.

How many people even know the names of our villages and camps which make up the tragic litany of nightmares that our people have endured since the creation of Israel in the heart of our ancestral homeland: Deir Yassin, Kalonia, Quibya, Kafr Qasim, Qalqilya, Nabi Elian, Azzun, Khan Unis, Sammu, Tel al-Zaatar?

It was at Deir Yassin that Menachem Begin inaugurated his doctrine that any act can be justified by its success. At dawn on April 9, 1948, while the Palestinian village on the outskirts of Jerusalem slept, 200 members of Irgun, the Zionist terror gang, attacked. House by house, the inhabitants were pulled into the street, lined against walls and shot, regardless of age or sex. Homes were dynamited. The attackers raped, tore earrings from women's ears and slaughtered some who were pregnant with carving knives. When day broke, corpses littered the streets.

No one was allowed into the village except a Jewish policeman, who reported that one Palestinian had died. It took a persistent Red Cross officer to unearth the truth. Besides the bodies in the streets, he found 150 corpses stuffed down a well. In all, 243 were left dead.

The survivors were stripped naked and paraded through a Jewish quarter of Jerusalem, to be mocked and spat upon. The then-leader of Irgun is now the prime minister of Israel.

In October 1953, Ariel Sharon led a similar operation against the unsuspecting inhabitants of Qibya, leaving 75 dead and as many wounded. Now Defense Minister Sharon defends his authorization to let his allies enter Sabra and Chatila by claiming to have warned against killing, "especially women and children."

Neither in their objectives nor in the morbid detail do the Beirut massacres differ from the carnage we have previously endured. Is not the mass murder of Palestinians consistent with the cold logic of Zionism, which dictated the destruction, expulsion or, at best, oppression of the indigenous people of the coveted land?

To us Palestinians, these dangers are not a mere abstraction. Ask the refugees who fled their homes in the panic of terror and war, never to be allowed to return. Or the young people who saw compatriots die under Israeli bullets for the crime of marching in peaceful demonstration. Or the librarians who have watched helplessly as the contents of their shelves were ransacked by Israeli police. Ask the orphans of Deir Yassin, Sabra and Chatila, who are unlikely ever to lead normal lives again.

We Palestinians cried out against this threat from our mosques and our churches, from the playgrounds of our schools and the courtyards of our homes, and, when in your more reflective moments you allowed it, from the columns of your newspapers and your airwaves. The world ignored our warnings. Now, thanks to modern communications technology, the massacre has taken place under your noses.

In its implacable campaign against us, Zionist propaganda stopped at nothing to deprive us of what was ours — our literature (we were depicted as aimlessly roaming bedouins), our history (Palestine, the most ancient country on earth, ceased to exist in their historical narratives), our geography (the cradle of human civilization — which grew fruit trees centuries before Europe, perfected irrigation and plant hybridization and was the first nation to produce such luxuries as wine — was presented to the world as strips of desert or malaria-ridden swamp). Thinking people everywhere should have known better; the world's ancient travelers and artists had testified otherwise.

As grim reports of the bloodbath in Sabra and Chatila flashed in, and the flickering screen featured Israeli soldiers rounding up our civilians, the leaders of a nation of "in-gathered exiles" disputed furiously in the Knesset over the fate of the original people. As a Palestinian, I felt as if I had been punched all over.

Scores of mutilated Palestinian bodies were displayed tied together so the victims could not flee, or slumped against a wall where they had been lined up and gunned down. As I looked on, vivid images of Deir Yassin and other calamities—both for the Jewish people and ourselves—flashed through my mind; but above all, images of our people's lives, our markets and ancient cities, exploding under the shells and bombs of Israeli soldiers.

As I watched, I wondered: What are the intentions of these people? What are they doing to our country, with its ancient customs and traditions, mosques and churches, legendary lakes and rivers, mystical hills and mountains?

When the debris of Sabra and Chatila is dug away, when the final toll of that Black Friday comes to light, let us also grieve for another victim—the smashed hope for coexistence between Israelis and Palestinians.

So much lost, so little left to lose. Will anyone now be surprised if, in our despair, the voices of people who once believed it possible to live side by side with the Israelis are stifled; if there is a rebirth of Palestinian extremism—indeed if there is an embittered, radicalized insistence that the Israelis have no place at all in our part of the world?

Guela Cohen, "Too Many Attacks on Jews in Palestine," *The International Herald Tribune*, Paris (Monday, October 14, 1982).

[The writer is a member of the Knesset from the Techiya Faction, a breakaway party from Likud that opposes the Camp David agreements. She responds here to Mohammad Tarbush, a Palestinian author whose comment after the Beirut massacres appeared on this page on Sept. 29 entitled "What Are the Palestinian People Supposed to Feel Now?"]

JERUSALEM—The "tragic litany of nightmares" that Mohammad Tarbush has cited in support of his questionable premise that Zionism is a disastrous doctrine is one-sided and far removed from the historical truth.

Mr. Tarbush claims Zionist logic "dictated the destruction, expulsion or, at best, oppression of the indigenous people" of Palestine. Well, what are the facts?

Zionism, as the national movement of liberation of the Jews, sought to re-establish political sovereignty in their ancient homeland. A Jewish presence was a constant factor in the history of the land of Israel, a land that had seen some dozen conquerors come and go since the first century of the common era. With the renewal of agricultural settlements more than 100 years ago to complement the

58

urban centers of Jerusalem, Hebron, Tiberias, Safad and others, Zionism entered the modern age as a political force, its raison d'être being to express a basic aim of Judaism: regained independence in the land of Israel.

During the early years of this return it would be more proper to say that the homecomers found the land under-populated. As Zionist enterprises opened up more employment opportunities and the health service improved with the draining of the swamps, the Arab population became anything but indigenous. Quite recent immigrants were from Egypt, Sudan, Syria, Lebanon and other areas, as can easily be verified by comparing the two British census reports. These point clearly to a rise in the urban population of Arabs, while village figures remained fairly level in accordance with natural increase.

The Jewish return was probably unique in the annals of humankind, in that the Zionists insisted on buying land. In contrast, it may be recalled how the Arabs had taken possession: In the third decade of the seventh century of the common era, tribes originating from the Hejaz region, recently converted to the new religion of Islam, subjugated most of the land of Israel.

Mr. Tarbush's claim that Palestine was an ancient Arab land goes to the heart of the conflict. The historical truth is that the accounts of many travelers all testify to the area's desolation and its lack of population.

Unpleasant as it is, one must also recall the all too many violent attacks on Jews in Palestine committed by Arabs: Jerusalem in 1920; Jaffa and Jerusalem in 1921; Jerusalem, Jaffa, Safad and the gruesome massacre of the old Yishuv non-Zionists in Hebron in 1929; the years of terror from 1936 to 1939 when more than 500 Jews were murdered, fields were burned, wells were blocked, transportation was ambushed and marketplaces were bombed. In many instances, in addition to the customary pillaging, raping and general mayhem, the victims were horribly mutilated. The some 130 villagers of Kfar Etzion who surrendered to Arab irregulars in May 1948 were summarily machine-gunned to death.

Deir Yassin? I personally know many of the Lechi and Irgun fighters who took part in the attack on Deir Yassin. The village overlooking the road to Jerusalem was decidedly not peaceful; not in 1948, nor certainly in 1920 and 1929 when the villagers participated in attacks on Jewish neighborhoods. Only five days before the combined Irgun-Lechi attack in 1948, the Histadrut newspaper, Davar, reported that again sniper fire from Deir Yassin had been directed at Jewish homes. The Haganah agreed that the village was of strategic importance and authorized the attack.

There was no raping. No one was lined up against a wall to be shot. No pregnant women were carved up. This is fiction.

What occurred at Deir Yassin was a battle. One-third of the attacking force was wounded by fire from the houses. Iraqi "volunteers" were found among the dead. Men dressed up in women's clothing and hid behind children. Despite warnings to leave the village (and indeed more than 200 people heeded them and escaped harm), many noncombatants were found in the houses, which were dynamited in the process of overwhelming the resistance.

Knowledge of whether those noncombatants were forcibly held there or not would lessen the grief, but it surely would alter the image of massacre that continues to be bandied about.

If the aim, according to Mr. Tarbush, was wholesale slaughter, why bother to parade live survivors? Indeed there was no such "parade," but the transfer of the rest of the villagers to Arab-held Jerusalem for their own benefit.

It is Mr. Tarbush's horrendous conclusion that there will be an "insistence that the Israelis have no place at all in our part of the world." He warns of a "rebirth of Palestinian extremism," but in fact this language of genocide and renewed holocaust is simply an extension of the common response of the Arabs of Palestine. As a child in the late 1930s I saw what irrational fury could do to my Arab neighbors.

But the faith that brought my mother's family from North Africa three generations before and the strength that enabled my father to walk from Yemen endure to help me defend my natural right, and that of my son and his generation, to live as a Jew in my homeland of Eretz Israel and to defend my life and goods in this period of Zionist revolution.

"In Palestine: Room for Debate?" *The International Herald Tribune*, Paris (Monday, October 25, 1982).

PARIS—If brute force is not to be the only rule in the Middle East, and if dialogue is ever to have its chance, then care will have to be taken with language. It is high time.

Theodor Herzl, the father of modern Zionism, wrote in 1895, "World history is nothing but noise, noise of arms and of advancing ideas. Men must put noise to use." Today in 1982, a Palestinian may be excused for judging that Israeli propagandists have had their way for too long.

Writing on this page on October 14, a member of the Knesset, Geula Cohen, continued to talk about Palestine as if its people did not and do not exist. It is legitimate to question the good faith behind such language, and the willingness to coexist peacefully with us.

No, the evidence is that the Palestinian presence does not begin in the 7th century with Hijazi tribesmen subjugating the land of Israel, as the Zionist line pretends, but that it goes back to 3000 B.C. and the Canaanites, the first known settlers in Palestine.

It was not Arabs but Romans who in 135 A.D. destroyed Jerusalem and killed or deported most of the Jews. And when Zionist immigrants started arriving in Palestine at the beginning of the present century, the country had a population of 700,000 [Arabs] owning 98 percent of the land.

So soon after the massacre of Palestinians in Beirut last month, to dismiss the 1948 Israeli massacre of Palestinians at Deir Yassin as a "battle" is a loud distortion of the documented truth. A member of the British investigating team, Richard Catling, reported that "Sexual atrocities were committed by the attacking Jews; many young girls were raped and later slaughtered." Erskine Childers told in The Spectator how captured villagers were "paraded through Jewish quarters of Jerusalem to be spat upon, then released to tell their kin of the experience."

Mrs. Cohen justified the raid on the village of Deir Yassin by "too many violent attacks on Jews." Indeed there had been attacks.

The context may be recalled. When Zionist immigrants arrived to create a Jewish state in a country where Jewish ownership of land was a mere 2 percent in 1918, their presence posed a real threat to the inhabitants. The process of settlement was characterized from the start by racial exclusivity.

Moshe Menuhin, father of the violinist Yehudi, wrote that he "could not stomach the daily preaching of 'our nation, our country, our birthplace' by our hypernationalistic, goyim-hating, Zionist Hebrew teachers. Not one of the students at the Gymnesia Herzlin was born in Arab Palestine. We all came to Palestine from Russia, Poland, Romania, Galicia, et cetera. The hatred and contempt for goyim—Arabs, in our case—was irrational and inhuman."

The Palestinians had no place in Zionist plans. David Ben-Gurion said that "Israel is the country of the Jews and only of the Jews."

Such words were systematically translated into deeds.

In 1948, when the Deir Yassin massacre sent terrified civilians fleeing in the naive belief that they would return to their homes and lands at the end of the hostilities, Jewish ownership of what is now Israel was still only 5.6 percent. But of the 370 kibutzim and other settlements established between 1948 and 1953, 350 are on the sites of destroyed Arab villages, including Beit-Natif, my birthplace.

If, as one still hears claimed, destruction, expulsion or oppression of Palestinians were not Zionist aims, questions suggest themselves for honest debate.

Why are the emergency and defense laws of 1945 and 1949 still in force, giving the state the right to detain civilians "for any reason whatsoever" for an unlimited period without trial and to expel them from the country and destroy or confiscate their property?

Why has Israel not heeded the United Nations, which since 1948 has called for the repatriation of Palestinian refugees?

Why were 18,000 Palestinian homes destroyed during the first seven years of Israel's occupation of the West Bank?

Why was the water supply systematically expropriated from Palestinian farmers so that by 1974, 50 percent of the cultivated land in the Jewish sector was irrigated, compared to 5 percent of the cultivated land in the Arab sector?

Why, 20 years after the creation of Israel, did 45 percent of the Palestinian population still not have access to electricity, when no Jewish settlement was without it?

Why do Palestinian workers receive less than half the pay of Jews for the same work?

Why is a Jew from anywhere entitled to Israeli citizenship and residence, when my compatriots and I whose ancestors inhabited Palestine for centuries, cannot share in that fundamental privilege?

Can Palestinians be blamed for not having welcomed the arriving Zionists in their land?

Today there are more than 4 million of us dispersed around the world, active in all walks of life. We will not simply disappear. For better or for worse, then, our destiny has been interlocked with that of the Israelis, and the continuing conflict is of concern to all.

Many of us are willing to let bygones be bygones, and advocate the effective partition of Palestine between Jews and Palestinians.

But perhaps in their very reasonableness these moderate voices are the main threat to extremist Israeli politicians, who thus try to drown them out with distorted versions of history. It is the responsibility of friends of both sides to prevent that tactic from succeeding.

"Arafat: Ready to Talk about Peace in Palestine," *The International Herald Tribune,* Paris (Wednesday, January 5, 1983).

PARIS — Salwa, a seaside hotel on the outskirts of Tunis, has been converted into the temporary headquarters of the Palestine Liberation Organization. In that unlikely setting a few days ago I met Yasser Arafat, chairman of the executive committee of the PLO, for the first time. It was past midnight when I was finally ushered into his office.

I have never belonged to any political organization, much less the PLO, but I knew Mr. Arafat's popularity among my fellow Palestinians. Most Israelis regard him as a terrorist. Many in the West have shared this view, at least until recently. Much of the world ranks him among the leading freedom fighters of the century. To most Palestinians he is simply the national leader.

Seen face to face at Salwa that night and on several succeeding nights, he came across like the head of a family whose youngest daughter has been kidnapped: Her release has become his raison d'être. He appears to be devoid of self-indulgence, an evidently religious man who eats and dresses simply, works hard and sleeps little.

A typical Arafat day is spent in official meetings in the morning, with some sleep in the afternoon and then organizational work through the night, interrupted by visiting delegations and the press.

This has also become the rhythm of life of many of the men, women, and children around him. It struck me, an outsider, that these abnormal hours contribute to making the man and his entourage disorganized.

Having lived in the West for the last 18 years, I was aware of the way Mr. Arafat is often projected in the media. I was going to ask why he never seemed to be clean-shaven, or why he insists on speaking to the Western media in his imperfect English, to the detriment of the ideas he tries to communicate. As we sat down to talk in Arabic, his bearing discouraged such questions as frivolous.

"I am an engineer forced to carry arms," he said. "I had a fortune in Kuwait, but with my country occupied it mattered little."

From his office, Mr. Arafat appears to follow in close detail almost any event concerning the Palestinian people, as well as listening to analysis of the international situation, to the latest news from "the front," to his comrades' accommodation problems and even to reports of their family wrangles.

This concern for people may explain his popularity. A Palestinian intellectual told me that Mr. Arafat is the only Arab leader who can walk among his people without fear.

Shortly before our meeting, Mr. Arafat had received a group of Norwegian photographers, who showed him slides of the massacre of Palestinian and Lebanese civilians at Sabra and Chatila. Recalling their visit, his eyebrows tightened as in a frown. He leaned forward and said quietly, "You should see the slides. Little girls raped and molested. Men's noses sliced away. The butchers cut off the fingers of those women victims wearing rings and took them away."

Violence has caused so much suffering on all sides in the Middle East, I offered.

"America did not honor its agreement with us," he said after a moment's silence. Through Philip Habib, it had accepted responsibility for the protection of Palestinian civilians and institutions as one of the conditions for PLO withdrawal from Beirut.

This was not Mr. Arafat's only source of disappointment with the United States. He said the Reagan administration had yet to free itself from the undertakings Henry Kissinger gave to Israel when he committed the Americans never to talk to the PLO. This in spite of the fact that Mr. Kissinger twice contacted the PLO through the Egyptian government during the 1976 civil war in Lebanon, when the PLO played a decisive role in protecting the American community in Beirut.

In Mr. Arafat's view, President Reagan assumed mistakenly that after Israel's invasion of Lebanon the PLO would be liquidated as a viable organization. Now, apparently, in their briefings to American officials America's friends in the Arab world and elsewhere have been telling them otherwise.

Did he then believe, I asked, that American foreign policy might be changing?

He seemed in no hurry to reply. I was disturbed by this silence, thinking that our meeting was coming to an abrupt end. I looked around for a distraction and was grateful for a knock on the door. It was a housekeeper coming to clear up the dinner plates. What did he have for dinner? I asked mechanically.

"Salad, bread, white cheese and honey," he answered looking rather surprised. "Americans care a lot about health food," I said, trying to pick up the thread of the conversation. He agreed, adding with satisfaction that the American public was becoming more conscious of the justice of the Palestinian cause.

He returned to my question. Alexander Haig perceived the Middle East in narrow militarist terms, he said. The Palestinians were a rock in the path of Mr. Haig's strategic designs. They simply had to go. "Like a construction engineer asking for the removal of obstructions from his working site, Haig conspired with the Israelis to wipe the Palestinians off the Middle East political map. But they underestimated our latent force. They forgot that even the most modern arsenal cannot defeat people armed with justice."

"I welcomed the arrival of Shultz," Mr. Arafat continued. Mr. Shultz seemed to recognize that the conflict is about real people, not objects to be shifted around. "But the American administration has yet to grasp the fact that without us, the Israelis will never be accepted in the Arab world."

"Even if Israeli soldiers roam the souks of Arab capitals, as they now do in Beirut, that will not make the Arabs accept them," Mr. Arafat said. "But I can even imagine Israeli children in our schools, Israeli nurses and doctors working in Arab hospitals, once the Palestinian problem is solved justly."

He characterized the Reagan plan as "positive," but compared it to "a car trying to run on three wheels—the missing element being recognition of the Palestinians' right to self-determination and to having their own state." He said the American administration should know by now that, in the Middle East, bilateral treaties alone could lead at best to the forging of diplomatic relations, but not normalization. "We are the key to acceptability and normalization," he said.

I told him my impression that the PLO tended to react to events rather than take the initiative. Why not act instead of react? He gave me the vague answer of a politician ("There are so many factors to balance. . ."), while insisting that there had been initiatives. The decision to accept a Palestinian state in the West Bank, for instance.

He said he was encouraged by the fact that important segments of Jewish public opinion, both in the West and in Israel itself, had come to see the need for a Palestinian settlement. "I would like to express my respect and admiration to the 400,000 Israelis who protested against the massacre," he said.

And then: "I am ready to be interviewed by Israeli television to talk about peace in Palestine. To discuss peace in Palestine, I welcome any Jew from anywhere."

I asked if he had a mandate from his organization to break this new ground. He told me the central committee had agreed to convene the Palestine National Council in Algeria toward the middle of February.

He said that in his efforts to press for a settlement based on a confederation between the future Palestinian state and Jordan, he had made significant progress toward rapprochement with King Hussein. In these efforts he said he had succeeded in mobilizing the support of the mainstream of Palestinian leaders and constituencies.

"Of course there are differences," he said, "but I am leading freedom fighters, not slaves. Everyone has the right to express himself. To test the popularity of our policies, let those in doubt hold an independent referendum, particularly among Palestinians living in the West Bank and Gaza."

As I stepped out the door into a corridor, a boy of four was running toward me in front of his mother. I blocked his way and said, using the Arabic word for nephew, "Where are you from, Amo?" "From Jaffa," came the matter-of-fact reply. [Presently his mother catches up with him. "Which one of you is the fighter?", I inquire. "Both of course," she answers with a smile. Then pointing to her son she adds; "But like all mothers, I don't want to bring him up as a fighter, or an exile." (unpublished)]

Letter: "Time to Lift the Western Veil on Islam," *The International Herald Tribune,* Paris (March 14, 1983).

PARIS — Judgements about the "Moslem world" can be as fatuous as judgments about the "Christian world," which takes in both Sweden and Paraguay. Moslems now number about a billion, dispersed around the globe.

They live in very different societies. A Moslem might have Aryan, Asian or African features. He might live in the wilderness of the Sahara or in cosmopolitain Beirut. Moslems include the stylishly dressed woman coming out of a cinema in Cairo, a beret-wearing farmer tending his vineyard in the south of France, a wanderer strolling through the souks of Fez in his loose *djellabiya.*

The complexity of the subject might explain the failure of the West to comprehend the Islamic world. But it often seems that this failure, particularly when it concerns the Arab region, is based on prejudice. Since the days of the Crusaders there has been a tendency in the West to view the Moslem Arab world with a caricaturizing mix of hostility and romanticism.

Still, it can come as a surprise to see a serious journalist misunderstand his subject. Such was the case in an article in this newspaper (Dec. 22) by David Lamb under the headline "Veil's Revival Reflects Women's Status in Islam."

The article was right to point out the unsatisfactory position of women in most Islamic societies. It suffered, though, from a failure to observe that the revival of Arab conservatism affects all sectors of society, male *and* female.

And why must Western observers look for a divine hand behind the veil? As evidence the article in question advances absurd quotations that it mistakenly attributes to the Koran.

No, the Koran does not promise men sexual relations (presumably with women, who might thus share in the fun) 72 times a day after death. It does not define women's role as biological. It does not advise on proper sexual positions. It does not prescribe women's clothing.

It does not regard women as sexual objects. A Moslem does not have the right to have intercourse with his wife without her consent.

And no, rape is not a serious problem in Cairo, nor in any other Arab city. The average incidence of rape in Arab cities is negligible compared to that in the safest of Western cities.

At about the time Christian missionaries were at work in Northern Europe 13 centuries ago, Islam came to the pagan tribes of Arabia as a civilizing agent. In the pre-Islamic period polygamy and the slave trade had flourished, women were considered a shame and female babies were buried alive, and excessive consumption of alcohol was a problem. As a practical religion Islam addressed itself to all aspects of social life.

It abolished slavery. It asked believers to refrain from alcohol, to wash before prayer and to refrain from eating meat, such as pork, that was subject to quick decay and infection.

It enhanced the status of women. A woman, Khawla Bint al-Azwar, became an army commander. The Prophet held that learning was a duty for every man and woman. Women such as Aisha, the Prophet's wife, and Isma, daughter of Caliph Abu Bakar, contributed significantly to Islamic culture. The delegation of 70 notables which in the 7th century endorsed the union between Mecca and Medina included 12 women.

Islam gave women the right to vote 13 centuries before Switzerland. In 1983 there are more women members (32) in the Palestine National Council than in Britain's House of Commons (19), which has a comparable number of seats.

The degrading practice of polygamy posed a serious problem. Old traditions and continuous wars, which took a heavy toll of the male population, provided arguments for maintaining it. Yet Islam discouraged polygamy; it insisted on almost impossible conditions, including equality among the spouses. Change continues, and Tunisia has abolished polygamy.

There were other deep-rooted traditions, including dress. One was the wearing of the "veil"—a black or white silk or cotton gown that covers a woman's head and extends down to the waist, knees or ankles, depending on age, region and customs. I am in no way an advocate of the veil, although I confess I have found it attractive, say, as worn by some women in Saudi Arabia over the latest haute-couture creations.

Like other aspects of life, the status of women varied with the rise and fall of the Islamic empire. At one point, of course, Arabic works were being translated into Latin and used as textbooks at the universities of Paris, Oxford and Louvain. It was from such heights that the Islamic empire slipped into the marshes of a decline from which the Arab world, the nerve center of Islamic civilization has never completely re-emerged.

In a number of today's fractious Arab states, suppression of basic freedoms for women and men is often the order of the day. Governments lacking legitimacy hide behind distorted versions of Islamic thought. But for the delinquency of such regimes Islam is no more at fault than is Christianity for despotism in Latin America.

And if some Egyptian women have discarded Western garments for conservative dress, it is also true that there are more women doctors per capita in Egypt than in the United States.

Paris

"Those (Not-Quite-So) Oil-Rich Arab Sheikhs," *The International Herald Tribune,* Paris (Tuesday, May 31, 1983).

PARIS—From the first gushings of the oil boom, Arab wealth has been resented. Above all, it has been exaggerated.

Even at the peak of the boom, the combined annual GNP of Saudi Arabia, Bahrain, the United Arab Emirates, Kuwait and Qatar, at close to $120 billion, was only slightly more than that of Belgium. The aggregate population of those five Arab countries—including foreigners, who in some cases make up as much as 50 percent—is only 11 million, a mere 7 percent of the Arab world's population.

To many citizens of the oil-producing countries, wealth arrived with the suddenness of a winning lottery ticket. Some were unable to deal with it rationally. The tales of unfettered shopping sprees are the stuff of well-documented legend. On the receiving end, too, there were abuses. Real estate prices in Europe invariably rocketed once hints of an interested Arab buyer began circulating.

Oil largesse was all the more resented because it arrived at a time when the West was feeling the pinch of its first major postwar recession. To Arab eyes it seemed that much of world opinion would have preferred the Gulf countries to remain dependent and backward.

The West expressed a genuine fear of this petro-wealth. Liquidity gave that wealth dynamic mobility and the power to stabilize or destabilize entire economies. Most Western economists would now agree that the governments of the oil-rich nations adopted a responsible line, going out of their way not to disrupt the world economy.

With their own economies capable of absorbing only so much of the new wealth, they invested as much as 60 percent of their surplus cash reserves in the West, most of it in negotiable deposits and short-term securities.

A major portion of their imports came from the West. Thus, the bulk of the oil revenues was recycled, directly or indirectly, to generate economic activity back in the industrial countries from which it had been earned. Interest payments may have boosted the "book value" of those Arab funds, but the real value has been reaped ultimately by the foreign banks, financial institutions and economic sectors that housed, borrowed or used those funds.

The largest Arab investors in the West have invariably been government agencies. With unmatched returns on their money at home, most private investors looked abroad more for security than profit. But both demonstrated a preference for easily convertible instruments such as Treasury bills or corporate bonds, leaving only a fraction of their capital for direct investment.

A recent report by Chase World Corporation estimates that direct investment by Arab governments and individuals represents less than 1 percent of all direct investments in the United States. It goes on to ridicule emotional outcries against the prospect of Arabs "buying up" America. It observes: "Only about 3 percent of U.S. farm acreage changes hands yearly; only 5 percent of the 3 percent is purchased by foreign buyers; and only 1 percent of the 5 percent of the 3 percent is bought by Arabs."

Now the shock of the recent drop in oil prices and accumulated experience and expertise are bound to produce a new orientation of Arab investment. The plummeting revenues have given a sharp reminder that oil reserves are non-renewable, and many Arab governments sense that this may be a pivotal time to develop their own economies.

So far they have concentrated on pouring their wealth into urbanization, industrialization and erecting an infrastructure of roads, airports and power stations. Out of the desert rose monuments to modern architecture — but also superfluous industrial schemes and acres of tacky apartment blocks and garish hotels that are already proving too costly to maintain and are destined to become ghost towns once the oil companies and their expatriate labor forces pack up to return home.

Just as the energy crisis of the '70s provoked Western governments into seeking a better way to manage their resources, the current squeeze on oil revenues may prompt Arab governments to become more vigilant with their own. Already there are reports that Arab oil-producing countries plan to spend no more than 60 percent of their current budgets — a far cry from the overruns of the '70s.

The crisis could also spark more serious thought about the economic needs and potential of the Arab world as a whole. While the oil-producing countries now contribute almost as much in international aid as the United States, in many Arab countries such basic amenities as hospitals, schools and sewerage systems are still lacking.

The United Nations ranks some Arab countries among the poorest countries in the world. In Egypt and Morocco, per capita income is still less than $800 a year. While the Arab world takes more than 10 percent ($32 billion) of the world's agricultural imports, only 30 percent of the arable land in the Arab world has been exploited.

Until now some Arab oil producers have allocated more than half of their annual budgets to defense. How wise an investment this is can be questioned, considering that none of them could rebuff a foreign attack without outside help, and that in some cases more than 75 percent of the national army is foreigners. National security might be better served by promoting the prosperity of their less fortunate Arab neighbors.

"A Tactless Coincidence—and an Opportunity," *The International Herald Tribune*, Paris (Tuesday, November 29, 1983).

PARIS—Today, November 29, happens to be International Solidarity Day for the Palestinian people. Friends around the world issue communiques reiterating support. Millions of people attend ceremonies, listen to Palestinian music and poetry, admire embroidery and other art works that generations have perfected down the centuries, taste Palestinian delicacies and watch traditional dances.

Friends have invited Palestinian leaders and academics to talk to them about Palestine, its culture, its people, their heritage, their achievements and their sufferings.

And today happens to be the day that Ronald Reagan receives Yitzhak Shamir. Mr. Reagan may be unaware of the coincidence.

Who is Prime Minister Shamir? Yitzhak Yzertinsky, as he then was, emigrated from Poland to Palestine in 1935. A disciple of the hard-line Zionism of Vladimir Jabotinsky, he joined the Irgun Zvai Leumi (National Military Organization) which tried unsuccessfully to forge an alliance with Mussolini.

Mr. Shamir and associates broke away from Irgun to found their own military organization,soon known as the Stern Gang. In 1940 they sought an alliance with Hitler.

(Lenni Brenner, the Jewish American author of *Zionism in the Age of the Dictators,* writing this fall in the London magazine *Middle East International,* quoted from their formal proposal as follows: "The establishment of the historical Jewish state on a national and totalitarian basis, and bound by a treaty with the German Reich, would be in the interest of a maintained and strengthened future German position of power in the Near East.")

Irgun and the Stern Gang competed in terrorism. Mr. Shamir's group assassinated Lord Moyne, the British resident minister in the Middle East. The two movements linked up in April 1948 to storm the Palestinian village of Deir Yassin, where some 250 civilians were massacred. In September 1948 the Stern Gang assassinated Count Folke Bernadotte, the United Nations mediator in Palestine.

Late last year Mr. Shamir was faulted by Israel's Kahan Commission for failing to act on news of the slaughter that was being perpetrated in the Palestinian camps of Sabra and Chatila in Beirut.

Today the fate of some 4 million Israeli Jews and as many Palestinian Arabs is in Mr. Shamir's hands.

A Palestinian would be entitled to observe that the epithet "terrorist" has been rather selectively applied over the years. Still perhaps the responsibilities of office can temper the most extremist of men. After half a century of extremism, Yitzhak Shamir may have turned over a new leaf when he agreed to the release of thousands of imprisoned Palestinians last week, thus bringing happiness to many families.

But if France,* with its relatively limited resources and influence, could engineer a coup de théâtre on that scale, what might not the United States do, if it chose?

It should be clear to all by now that peace will not come to Israelis and Palestinians unless the Israeli government withdraws its troops from the occupied Arab territories and recognizes the natural rights of Palestinians to self-determination.

The Reagan plan of September 1982 might have brought that about. The Israeli government resisted it, thereby condemning both the Reagan plan and the efforts of Palestinian moderate leaders, including Yasser Arafat, to failure.

Most Palestinians, whether Moslem or Christian, and surely some Israelis, must wish that it were Mr. Arafat who was the guest at the White House today.

---

*Editor's note: The French government played a decisive role in the negotiations that led to the exchange of Israeli and Palestinian prisoners referred to in the article.

"Arafat Is not Finished!" *Le Monde* (December 21, 1983).

PARIS — On a trip to the United States a few months ago, I was shocked though only mildly surprised to hear responsible Americans say that the game (as Mr. Reagan calls the Middle East conflict) was very simple. After Beirut and the dissidence at the heart of Fatah, one could write off Mr. Arafat. That is why the peace plan — a totally inadequate one, by the way — to which the President of the United States had given his own name, was totally neglected. Israel pursued its settlements policy in the occupied Arab territories. When Mr. Arafat and King Hussein were looking for a means of breathing life into the Reagan plan, the United States didn't lift a finger to support their efforts and lessen the risks that they were prepared to take.

Mr. Arafat was ready to risk his life, but on condition that Washington recognize the natural right of the Palestinian people to self-determination. Placing themselves decisively on the Israeli side, the Americans have chosen to ignore the basic cause of the Middle East conflict — that is, the Palestinian question — and to follow a short-term policy which would solve nothing. How much blood has been spilled since! How many orphans, widows, mothers and fathers have been devastated.

Is Mr. Arafat finished as the leader of the PLO, as the American government expected? Far from it. As the elected and legitimate leader of the PLO he is in the process of reinforcing his legitimacy. He has the support of the Palestinians in the occupied territories and in the diaspora and of the majority in the Palestine National Council. There have been many popular demonstrations of support for him, but none for his adversaries, even in the camps which *they* control.

The organization which he controls will no doubt reach its apogee in the near future. If the powerful armies of Israel and Syria have not succeeded in liquidating the PLO, it would be futile for others to try. Fire hardens what it cannot destroy. Let us recall the recovery or the significant evolution of the PLO, in spite of the numerous attempts to destroy it: 1968 at Karameh, 1970 at Amman, 1976 at Tel-Al-Zaatar and, finally, 1982 at Beirut. Obviously in the course of its growth the PLO has become, like all organizations which involve thousands of people, difficult to control. There have been excesses, even abuses; its leaders have committed indiscretions and errors.

At times neither its use of time nor the behavior of its emissaries abroad has conformed with what might be expected of the leadership of a revolutionary movement. In spite of this, the PLO has succeeded in creating democratic procedures which suggest the possibility of a progressivist evolution. It is these procedures which the dissidents would have followed, had they represented a truly authentic movement, instead of turning their guns on their Palestinian comrades.

Attempts at conciliation inside the PLO, followed by the dispatch of emissaries from the executive committee to the dissident groups, demonstrated the democratic will of Yasser Arafat. It is in this sense that the dissidents, in aligning themselves with Syria, have exiled themselves — de facto — from the PLO. The PLO has not been transformed into an instrument of repression, in spite of the historical opportunity offered by its enemies to refuse to negotiate and to physically eliminate the dissidents.

Paradoxically, the PLO is today the victim of the authenticity of its democratic structures.

What lessons can be drawn from these latest events? Contrary to the predictions, which proliferate like weeds, the tragedy of Syrian intervention belongs above all to the history of the formation of the Palestinian national consciousness. Syria can only be the loser in the chess game being directed by the United States and Israel. In insisting on placing the Palestinian people under its authority, Syria is losing all credibility in the Arab world and, to a certain extent, among the non-aligned nations. Syria is fomenting an increasingly virulent internal opposition; this situation will inevitably be exploited by Israel and the United States.

The convergence of short-term interests between Syria and the Israeli-American coalition will founder when it no longer serves the coalition's purposes. Syria remains above all the enemy of Israel and its allies, beyond the temporary expedient alliances concerning Lebanon.

At bottom, Assad and Shamir share at least one common characteristic: they each conduct short-term policies of devastating consequences.

It does not take a genius to understand that the essence of the Middle East conflict since the creation of Israel has not changed: it is the Palestinian question.

The attempts, from wherever they arise, to destroy the PLO can only serve to increase its radicalism: whence the murderous political violence of Jerusalem. "Who will be able to control our militants if my diplomatic efforts for a just settlement fail?" Mr. Arafat asked in an interview several months ago.

Instead of becoming mired in digressions, of emphasizing its archaic imperialism, of setting up bogus threats (the Soviet Union and Syria) Israel would do better to try to finally resolve the question of the occupied territories, an essential step which must sooner or later be seriously addressed.

But a significant part of the Israeli ruling class remains faithful to the dogma of Vladimir Jabotinsky and dreams incessantly of the resurrection of Greater Israel. And Mr. Shamir is a distinguished disciple of this tendency.

"Frustration with America Is Growing," *The International Herald Tribune*, Paris (Thursday, October 4, 1984).

PARIS — If the cycle of violence that has recently ravaged Lebanon — not just the attack on the U.S. Embassy in Beirut, but also attacks on the entourage of a Lebanese cabinet minister, on Palestinian and Lebanese refugee camps and on a convoy of Israeli buses — is not to suck in more bystanders, then an in-depth appraisal of existing policies and a serious search for new approaches is called for. The White House could set a much-needed example.

Tired are the voices that warn that U.S. policy in the Middle East is leading all involved into a dangerous dead end. Opponents are multiplying in number; the depth of their feeling is made obvious by abhorrent, self-sacrificing acts. Their militancy has many causes, good and not so good. It is rooted in a profound sense of injustice magnified by American blunders and Israeli insensitivity.

What are America's Arab friends to say when they see the U.S. government stifle criticism at the United Nations of the Israeli army's occupation of southern Lebanon — criticism that even Israelis are free to make? The United States has called for a freeze on Jewish settlements in occupied territories, but what has it done to bring about such a freeze? Why did Washington remain silent when Israel promulgated new laws making it possible for its military courts to condemn a West Bank stone-thrower to up to 20 years in prison?

Arab leaders have given many American administrations opportunities to switch to more evenhanded policies. But these leaders and their people seem to be taken for granted by American politicians.

Analysts have often attributed American failures in the Middle East to lack of knowledge and experience of the area, but this is no longer true.

George Shultz's appointment to the State Department was welcomed by several Arab leaders, including Yasser Arafat. In the view of the Palestinian leader, Mr. Shultz seemed to recognize that the Middle East conflict was about real people. But Mr. Shultz is now perceived as having consolidated America's almost unconditional support for Israel, with little regard to the national feelings and interests of Arabs.

Mr. Shultz's arrival in July preceded announcement on September 1, 1982, of the Reagan plan for Middle East peace. Arab leaders met in Fez, Morocco, on September 9, ultimately releasing their own peace proposals. It would be surprising if U.S. intelligence services had no previous knowledge of the Fez peace proposals.

The unanimously adopted Fez plan recognized the right of all states to live in peace. It contained concessions that the West had been asking the Arabs to make toward Israel.

By pre-empting the Fez summit with the Reagan plan, Washington contributed to the Arab world's regression back into the disarray it had been suffering from for so long. The short-lived unity achieved at Fez was undone amid the bullets of Syrians, Palestinians, Libyans and others fighting each other in Lebanon.

Nor was it long after Mr. Shultz's arrival at the State Department that the U.S. Navy could be seen bombarding targets in Lebanon.

Reasons for frustration with U.S. Middle East policy are many. What is surprising is the rapid spread of this frustration among wordly and well-educated Arabs. As a banker I rub shoulders with leaders of the Arab business community. Apart from finance, politics is always a favored subject. I can testify to a shift of attitude among this class. At the beginning of the oil boom, most of these businessmen were hypnotized by the excitement of big money. Now many are questioning the true value of their material comfort and new luxuries in the absence of national dignity.

A Palestinian told me how after becoming a refugee in 1948, he went to work in one oil-rich country. "Since then I have played an important role in building what you can see around me," he said. "Yet a teen-age immigration officer can ask me to justify my presence in his country."

"I own many houses and apartments all over the world, but I do not have a home," he added.

"A Palestinian Answer to a Fundamental Question," *The International Herald Tribune,* Paris (Saturday-Sunday, March 9-10, 1985).

PARIS—A question often put to Palestinians is, Why not do as other refugees have done and adopt the countries you now live in?

Even if one ignores the weakness of comparisons in a fair analysis (they tend to oversimplify issues), not to mention the moral points that might be brought to bear, there are aspects of the Palestinian problem that make it altogether different from others involving refugees.

In other instances in which war or upheaval has displaced masses of people, it has usually been possible for the displaced to regain their homes—or at least the right to reestablish them in the same city, the same country. The social and political climate might have changed. Perhaps even the geographical environment might be different. But historically, the victims of war and famine could go back to their soil.

Masses of Sicilians might emigrate to America, impelled by economic considerations; Poles might defect; Ethiopians might cross into Sudan in search of food; Cambodians might take to rafts to escape torture and starvation.

The immigrants might choose to stay, and the children and grandchildren of those storied huddled masses are probably materially richer for their ancestors' decision to remain in America, not to mention the dynamism they gave that country. Or the displaced might not choose to stay and they might face political reprisals for returning home. But Sicily is still Sicily and Poland is still Poland. It is even a reasonable expectation that someday the millions who have fled Cambodia's sad and torturous system will be able to return in peace.

Not so with Palestinians. A conscious, systematic effort is not just keeping us off our lands; it is trying to erase our identity and our country's identity from human memory.

The land is officially called Judea and Samaria by the occupying Israelis. Even the words "Palestine" and "Palestinian" do not exist in Israeli school textbooks.

Palestinian traditions have been rebaptized. Falafel, a popular Palestinian dish, is now presented to the world as an Israeli delicacy. Palestinian embroidered dresses are worn by El Al hostesses as symbols of Israeli craft. It is just so much Dead Sea salt in festering sores.

The first wave of refugees left Palestine during the 1948 war. Another exodus, also driven by fear, followed the 1967 war. Almost three million of the total Palestinian population of four million are now refugees or exiles. When hostilities died down after both wars, the refugees were kept from returning. Even the annual United Nations call for their repatriation goes unheeded.

All this is familiar, of course. The situation has been discussed and described in the media for decades. But because it is still unresolved, because the issue is so crucial to peace in the Middle East and because the human dimensions get lost in the rhetoric and the statistics, let me cite an example, the case of my own family. I come from a land-owning family that lived in Beit-Natif, a biblical village 16 kilometers (10 miles) west of Bethlehem.

To my forebears, not only was land the main source of livelihood, but the agricultural seasons were the pivot of the family's traditions and customs. Their deep attachment to the land and its produce is reflected in the touching gesture of christening old fig, almond and olive trees as if they were branches of the family. Quite naturally these people resisted all pressures to sell their land to anyone.

When the fear and panic that prevailed in Palestine in 1948 sent them running east, their main concern in their new abodes was to find ways to return to their land. That was not to be, and even their humble new home in Jericho had to be abandoned during the 1967 war.

It was from Jericho that I came to Europe in 1964 as a student. When the war erupted in June 1967, Jericho fell under occupation and my family again had to flee. As soon as the war stopped I made every effort to secure my right to return to Jericho, which had been my family's refuge of nearly 20 years, or to Beit-Natif, our personal homeland.

In the process, I corresponded for several months with the Israeli Embassy in London, and through them with the immigration authorities in Jerusalem. When that failed, I wrote about our case in *The Times* of London in February 1972. Two years later an eminent Jewish professor of juris-prudence at Oxford University took the matter up with Shmuel Toledano, then Prime Minister Golda Meir's ad-viser on Arab affairs. All was to no avail.

My father's most cherished wish before he died in 1982

was to be buried in Beit-Natif, where he was born and our ancestors are buried. Before 1947, shifts in power in Palestine had little bearing on my family. When the Ottoman empire crumbled and Palestine slipped under British rule after World War I, my family switched to paying their land levies to the British authorities. Ottoman land deeds and British tax receipts now decorate the walls of my study. They are still documents proving our ownership of a land that we neither sold nor wish to sell.

"An Arab Case for Peace with Israel," *The International Herald Tribune*, Paris, (October 14, 1985).

PARIS—After the attack on Tunisia, Arab leaders reacted to Israel's violation of the sovereignty of yet another Arab state with the usual rhetoric. Their publics observe such theatrics with disdain, asking cynically how many Israeli casualties have fallen victim to the latest assault of Arab verbal missiles.

After the creation of Israel in 1948, while its successive governments settled down to real business, creating more and more "facts" every day, Arab leaders developed a reflex that has become a ritual. Rather than take any measures that might ultimately undo or at least contain some of these "facts," they content themselves with issuing "strongly worded" protests that warn the enemy against "dire" consequences.

What the victims of aggression mostly need is concrete action, a helping hand they can touch, not a pledge of any country's ink and paper resources.

Arab rhetoric has been as harmful to the Palestinians as Israel's phosphoric bombs and F-15s. It provided Israel with the national cohesion it so badly needed. It became an endless source of the propaganda material that Israel has used so well for cultivating the sympathy of Western public opinion. More tragically, it has led to the demoralization of the Arab people.

Preparations for the proclaimed battle of liberation have gone on forever. Costly and sophisticated arsenals have been bought and left to rust in warehouses. Arab soldiers are entrenched around their capitals ready to crush any internal threat to their rulers, as the national borders remain open to outside adventurers.

Israel fought wars and won them. It displaced more people and acquired territory three times its original size. It made Jerusalem its capital and violated the so-called sovereignty of Arab states as it pleased — all of this without one Arab leader resigning from office for failure to protect the national interest; all without a toning down of the jarring rhetoric; all without halting the outflow of strongly worded messages. Having lost faith in the leadership, the average Arab is now apathetic, more interested in simple survival or, in favored cases, in accumulating wealth that neither he nor his descendants could ever live long enough to spend.

Of course, such a state of affairs could only be transitional. But it might be years before this hypnotized lion starts stirring again.

In the meantime it would be more dignified for the leaders of the Arab world to make peace with Israel, if only because they cannot, indeed will not, make war. Future generations will curse them for treason in signing away a sacred part of their native land. None will have a monument bearing his name in the market square. But this course of action, which might put an end to human sufferings and tragic losses of life, is certainly more honorable than the barrage of humiliating blows being delivered to the

Arab people with every Israeli invasion and bombardment.

Above all, a settlement of the Palestinian problem would deprive Arab regimes of a pretext for blocking out serious reforms and suppressing basic liberties.

For Israelis, peace remains the biggest threat to national cohesion. With no external threat, imagined or real, holding their social structure together, deep-rooted contradictions within their heterogeneous society will surface and ultimately undermine the stability of the state. Zionism will at last manifest its futility.

For the Palestinians, to give up a slice of their traditional homeland will never be acceptable, but in the long term they can only benefit from a new situation that might bring the Arab world out of its present stagnation and deprive the Israelis of a ready pretext for manipulating world opinion and for committing all kinds of violations in the name of national security.

Mohammad Tarbush was born in mandated Palestine. In the aftermath of the 1948 war his family became refugees and finally settled in Jericho on what became known as the West Bank. After attending school in Jericho, he went to Europe, where he studied in Italy, Switzerland and, finally, in England, at the universities of Durham, London, and Oxford. He is the author of *The Role of the Military in Politics: A Case Study of Iraq to 1941*. Dr. Tarbush now lives with his wife Huda and son Bassel in Paris, where he is working as an investment banker. He is also the Chairman of the Board of Trustees of the United Palestinian Appeal (UPA), a non-profit, non-political, tax-exempt charity based in Washington, D. C.